WHISPERS OF THE MOONLIGHT

RAJNANDNI KUMARI

Dedicated to everyone who loved & never loved.

Contents

Contents

1. Reality?

To live is to exist, but to exist is to not live but we are still existing even if we don't want to exist, still breathing but not living, living but dying, smiling when crying, living dreams in the frame of reality, existing in virtually, breathing in trances, crying in validity, smiling in vision.

So the question is we existing or living?

2. Dreamy

I always think about you,

I stole you from my dream.

Believe it or not.

You make me dream

in my dreams.

3. Tears

The star would
be shining.

The moon
would be shy.

The shine falls
in your smile.

You're beauty,
You're crazy.

Like tears,
you're always in my eyes.

4. Redeyes

Tired and red eyes,
saw the dream
with heavy sights.
Fill the potion of faith
in my vacant eyes,
fall of tears loves me,
in the middle of the night.
See the emotions,
in my glossy eyes.
Salvage my tears,
like a knight.
Calm sits in,
my stormy eyes.
With fiery passion,
never felt so right.
Love swims in,
my lonely eyes.
Telling me how
pain feels like.

5. Heart

You smile at me,

when we meet,

my heart says,

let's skips a beat.

6. Beat

You shine like the sunshine,
When you will
going to be mine?

You are the cold in the rain,
When your coldness
will ease my pain?

You are the beat of the heart,
When your heart will
beat for my heart?

7. Infatuation

Etch of your fingertips
shine on my hips,
like the smell of
cigarettes on your lips.
Wants to float, in your light.
Like the moon shines,
in the sunlight.
Is it love or infatuation?
Tears said you are nothing
but my destruction.
Swimming in your intoxication,
Devouring you like
my favourite medication.
Love the touch of yours,
It gives me sensation.
Wrote our love in the,
form of illustration.

8. Phony

When I look at you,

words meet end,

Your eyes tell me not to fear,

it's not the end.

9. Stitches

Delicate doll carved with knife,
The Sombre doll wants to
breathe life.

Eyes releasing the tears,
Not gazing at everyone
with fear.

Emotions are shredded into pieces,
heart breathing to
survive with stitches.

NEVER
FOREVER

10. Forever

You told me,
you love me.
Uncertainty says,
this love will end me.
You wore the
mask of forever,
behind the emotion
of never.
You built the
house of dream,
leaving me alone for
the midnight scream.
You told me
you'll be here,
I knew that,
you'll disappear.
You picked me
up from falling,
and I knew one day
you'll ignore my calling.

11. Sweet

You are the petal

of my flower,

Pour the love of yours

on me like a shower.

12. Love

You held me when I was falling,
but you never know that
am still falling.

You wiped my tears,
when I was in fear.

You told me, it's ok to break,
Because you will
always keep me safe.

13. Chained

Chained my,
broken heart,
fearing love,
won't fall apart.
Emotions get more vulnerable.
Making my eyes
uncomfortable.
I smiled and said it's fine,
but deep down
my heart says
nothing is fine.
I shushed my heart
says keep quiet.
My heart says time will
tell you nothing is right.
We both sighs and said
let it be all we can do is
burn this candle in
this dark light.

14. Shiny

Don't leave me alone,

I'll be there for you.

Like the sun,

I'll shine for you.

15. Storm

The place for you
is in my heart,
leaving you induce
pain in my heart.

Your touch feels like
the softness of sky,
leaving you brings
the storm in my eyes.

My love for you is
always be in me,
If you leaving
please, take the key.

16. Rain

Sitting in the park,
Rain pouring in
the dark.
My life turns grey,
Stuck in this life
like a prey.
Loneliness walks on my
life like a runway,
Waiting for love to
light my way.
People call her insane,
Because she looks for
her love in rain.

17. Heavenly

You are the soft duvet

that keeps me warm.

I feel like heaven,

when I'm in your arms.

18. Death

Laying on the death sheet,
Heart is beating
with the dead beat.

Finding comfort in
the crying heat,
people called you weak beat.

When you find
comfort in,
the death sheet.

LOVE

19. Fae

Love is throwing yourself
into a stormy sea.
Hoping there are
arms to catch me,
when I'll bleed.
Without the leap,
you're leaving me to bleed.
Bring me a love basket,
When you will
visit to my casket.
Laying in the arms of grave,
curling up with your memory,
I will be safe,
love is magical just like fae.

20. Merged

The distance between us

can't keep us apart,

we are merged like

the colours in the art.

21. Light

Loved you at first sight,
Holding our
love tight.

Heart waiting for
your love,
with the candle light.

Loving you felt
so much right.

Losing you makes,
my eyes bleed
in the midnight.

22. Game

I wrote under
the sky,
I write for
your eyes.
Your love got
me hypnotize.
My heart
gets mesmerized.
Our hearts says,
we have some ties.
The feeling which,
no emotion can deny.
Playing with our tears
like fierce game.
Loving with no love
all we do play is
blame game.

23. Felt

Felt your emotions,

and love like a sweet touch.

Knew the feeling of want,

would be too much.

24. Faux

The way people change,
just like the
season change.

Can't decide what
is more colder,
People or the weather?

Can't decide what
is more real,
Feelings or the
faux leather?

25. Silk

Wrapped my heart,
in soft silk.
You stained my heart,
with love ink.
Stoled my tears,
with a wink.
Devoured your feelings,
with one drink.
You look like a dream,
in my heavy blinks.
My love boat
reached you,
don't let it sink.

26. Charming

The charms of your

heart I can't resist,

With the presence of you,

I know love can exist.

27. Stars

Spent night in
your arms,
under the sky
full of stars.

Never knew it
was false of
the stars.

Like the fake
warmth of
your arms.

28. Calling

Everyone loves talking,
No one loves listening.
The sound of,
peace is shrilling.
Every breath makes,
the situation thrilling.
Heart said the,
beat is calling.
told that don't worry,
it's just a feeling.
Every tears are rolling,
Dreams shatter with a sigh,
When the tears realise
it was nothing but an
illusion of my darling

29. Love

My hand in your hand,

You can take the lead,

With your love and devotion,

I promise to follow your every lead.

30. Blind

Your love blossoms
flower in
my mind.

Like every beautiful flower,
You are
one of a kind.

Your love gave me heart eyes,
For your love
my heart is blind.

31. Ocean

My heart is the ocean,
You're my boat.
My feelings burning in blue,
Feeling your
emotion in hue.
Waves are my heartbeat,
Sending ripples in
your heartbeat.
Drown in me, drive into me,
Live with me,
bleed for me.
Turn the blue into yellow,
Make the ocean burn
like summer glow.

32. Burned

Love is just

like a cigarette.

Cigarette burns the lungs

and love burns the heart.

33. Smile

You are you, I have you,
You say you are nothing
For me, you are everything.

If you hate your heart,
Give me a chance,
to love your heart.

Let me kiss your tears,
Please smile when
you look at the mirror.

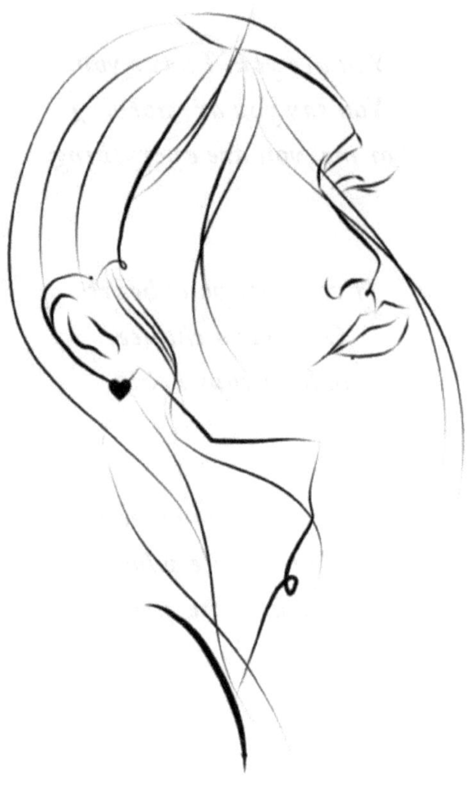

34. Cigarettes

Inhale your love,
my lungs
savour it.
My heart
burns like,
it's favourite hit.
Shipped my love
to you, and it's
still in transit.
Got addicted to
your touch,
like a nicotine.
I crave you
like cigarettes,
darling let
me breathe you in.

35. Tied

Staying in your arms,

my breathe get tied.

Feeling the feel of you,

my life get tied.

36. Arms

My emotions are apostate,
making my
heart suffocate.

You crying in my arms,
trying to make you
feel warm.

Your emotions
fill me with distrust.
I'm writhing in disgust.

Your heart fell for someone,
every feelings
goes undone.

37. Wish

Wish I could know,
what scares you.
Wish I could steal,
the loneliness from you.
Wish I could say,
love is a waste.
Wish I could say,
It's waste like trash.
Wish I could say,
this lips never knew you
Wish I could say,
this heart never meant
to love you.
Wish I could know,
how to never love you.

38. Boxed

You left me with the emotions,

that made my heart hiss.

I vow to box your love,

forever on my fingertips.

39. Comfort

You chased the shadow,
Making me
feel hollow.

Breathing the feel in low,
Heart blushing
in sad glow.

Need your comfort
like a pillow,
floating in the
arms of willow.

Forever
Together

40. Polaroid

Simmer of your gaze,
burned inside me
like a rage.
Never understood
the love language.
You taught me
love has no language.
Savor you like
my favorite beverage.
You hug my
heart like salvage.
Captured our love,
in Polaroid image,
Together we will write
forever in our love page.
Shakespeare told
life is a stage,
My heart says we will
End together on this stage.

41. Written

The wish of my heart is

written on my lips,

Can your heart able to

read that wish?

42. Lonliness

Heart is bleeding,
eyes are crying,
pain just cant go away.

Loneliness is a bed
where my heart
sleeps daily.

It's just wants love and
care this what the
soul scream.

Tough to breathe people provoke
your eyes to shades
some tears.

Is it too hard to listen
to the breathe of heart?

43. Moonlight

Whisper of the moonlight,
always starts when
we kiss under
the moonshine.
Loved the touch,
under the sheets.
Saved every moment,
when our eyes meet.
I can feel the,
rush of adrenaline.
Can't even narrate,
the way our love is defined.
Felt like knew you
from the beginning
Can't believe our love
book is already ending.

Rajnandni Kumari

Rajnandni Kumari is a poet, writer and artist. She is creative and has a very imaginative soul. She has always been enthusiastic about writing, and she's privileged to have turned her never-ending imagination into words. Writing has always been an escape from reality for her. People love their dream because it's different from the reality they are living in it and her reality is molded in such a way that all she want is to break every piece of her reality. She has written prolifically and is constantly exploring the world of words. In a mess of reality, she's happier when she sits down at her desk putting the opening words to her indistict mind.

Email : kumarirajnandni29@gmail.com

9 798887 721422

Printed by Libri Plureos GmbH in Hamburg,
Germany